Pregnant? Push!:
Birthing God's Purpose For Your Life

By: Chakita Hargrove
Foreword By: Ellenar Harper

Heart Ink Press LLC

Heart.Ink Press, LLC
P.O. Box 6312
Tallahassee, FL 32314

"Manifesting Dreams and Visions…
…Tuned to the Beat of Your Heart"

ISBN: 978-0-9823814-1-0
ISBN: 0-9823814-1-7
Copyrighted © by Chakita Hargrove

C o n t e n t

C h a p t e r s

Dedicated To:

Ellenar Harper
(referred to as roommate)

Foreword

I've always said that our friendship was the result of divine intervention.

Sometimes when two people meet for the first time their chemistry just seems to work. I'll never forget the Father's Day in 2002 when I met Chakita in room 411 of the Jennie Murphee Hall at Florida State University our freshman year. Although we were grouped as roommates according to the spelling of our last names, the encounter was kismet. I remember telling 'Kita, as I would later call her, while standing in front of her Chester drawer that she was going to be my new best friend, that I was going to follow her wherever she went whether she liked it or not, and that she wasn't going to get rid of me. And almost instantly, I clung to her side. I became her shadow, sort of speak. And she let me.

Our friendship and connection grew strong rather quickly, and we developed a sincere, genuine love. A sisterly love. We looked out for one another. More truthfully, rather Kita looked out for me.

Although she doesn't take too kind to excuses, or any type of foolishness, she's simple at heart and easy to get along with. Kita has a deep compassion for the children of God and unbelievers alike. The unselfish approach she has when it comes to caring for others, their well-being, and their soul salvation is admirable. Her mother-like aura is the exemplar of her personality - nurturing, providing, guiding, loving unconditionally, disciplining, strengthening, reinforcing, protecting.

More important, she has an appetite for the Truth. Often times she tells it like it is, straight no chaser, especially in regards to spiritual things. There's no sense in sugar-coating things that matter to the soul's salvation, right? When it comes to the Gospel and preaching the Word, a lackadaisical attitude will not suffice. For Kita, it's all or nothing. And in this book she definitely puts it all out there.

Her wisdom, as revealed in the following pages, eludes her age. She's young, but she has much experience which she has gained through trials and errors, through tests, and storms, tribulations, and temptations. Some of them she unashamedly speaks about in depth. Others are mentioned in passing. But she doesn't (and never has) complain or even boast about what she's suffered or gained. The anecdotes she shares are not for acclaim, but for the glory of God. That one soul may be inspired to take the charge God has given him or her, to pass the torch, to press forward, to live a Christ-centered life, to preach the undiluted Gospel, to stand upright for what *is* right, to be forthcoming, to be fearless, to be faithful, to be prayerful, or to be or do just a little bit better than before is her sole purpose.

Her words are written with sincerity, nostalgia, and urgency, as well as with optimism. There's a no nonsense approach to her genre, or style of writing. An approach that's sensible and easy to relate to. Kita doesn't talk at the reader; she speaks *to* the reader with tenderness, as I imagine Christ would have spoken to the twelve disciples, because she is concerned about his or her personal relationship with Christ while on this Christian journey.

 She is concerned about the betterment of the Lord's kingdom. She is concerned about the work of the Lord and filling His will, the will He has for her life, my life, your life, the lives of others, and the purposes for which we were created to perform.

Be prepared to constantly re-evaluate yourself with the flip of each page. *Pregnant? Push!* is exceedingly thought provoking and discusses issues that are virtually taboo for ministers or prophets and prophetesses to utter, issues that are perhaps outside your comfort zone, issues, nonetheless, that ignite change and speak hope. Issues that may cause *your* water to break!

Foreword by Ellenar Harper

Preface

It is evident through the reading of God's word that with every promise, some form of trial will come. With every elevation in kingdom work, some type of test will be given. With every purpose, you will have to be tested. These things are necessary in order to make you strong enough to handle where God is taking you. Being tried, tested and put through trials serve as pre-requisites in receiving God's plan, purpose and destiny for your life.

How can you handle the magnitude of God if your character, motive, and attitude are wrong? Why would God want to elevate you to your full potential in the kingdom if you don't know how to serve, submit, remain humble and tame your tongue?

Pregnant? Push!: Birthing God's Purpose For Your Life was written to encourage individuals who are having a hard time understanding why they are experiencing so much pain, loneliness, and inconsistencies in their walk with Christ. This book is also for those who are running from God's calling on their life; they feel God tugging but they refuse to give in.

Through responding "yes" to God's call and letting Him know that I am available, ready and willing to be His vessel, I unknowingly submitted myself to trials. God had to teach me who he really is. He had to reveal some things that He had planted in me since the beginning of my time here on earth. He had to take me through trials and tribulations to see if my motives were right. He had to make sure that I didn't say "yes" just so that I could be internationally known. He had to break me from old thought patterns. He had to heal me from family and church hurt. He had to reveal hidden truths and correct wrong teachings. He had to put me in a place where it was just Him and me.

While in this process of birthing what God had placed in me I had to lose all that I had. I had to be humbled, positioned and prepared for where He was, and is, taking me. Though I wanted to quit, I couldn't because of you.

Back in 2004 when I accepted my ministry calling to preach, teach and prophesy, God told me then that I will be His true example of a minister. And because God has put me in a place where I have mentees and youth constantly tugging at me, I can't quit.

While reading through *Pregnant? Push!: Birthing God's Purpose For Your Life,* you will learn of some trials I had to go through and of some tests I had to experience that were essential to birthing my purpose. With every dream and with every vision, you will have contractions. These contractions will help you in order to push your dreams and visions into the birth canal for manifestation.

I am here to encourage you and let you know that…

you can't quit pushing!

-Chakita Hargrove

Definition of Purpose

Purpose (n)

1. The object toward which one strives or for which something exists; an aim or a goal.

2. A result or effect that is intended or desired; an intention.

3. Determination; resolution

4. The matter at hand; the point at issue

Chapter 1

"For many are called, but few are chosen."
-Matthew 22:14

Chapter 1: Accepting God's Purpose

There are many people who are called to do marvelous things in this world and show the greatness of God through living as true examples of His word through preaching, teaching, mentoring, encouraging others and so much more. Many avenues can be used to show God's trueness and the miracles He has been known to perform in the biblical days. Somewhere in years past we have forgotten that before Jesus went to heaven to be with His father, He said, "Greater works than these shall ye do." Where has our faith gone? Because this world is populated with billions of people, I will say that only a quaint few really exemplify and live in faith the words Christ spoke while roaming the earth.

When I was ten years old I started to realize that I was different from other children my age. I didn't enjoy playing on the playground, talking on the phone, or spending long hours outside playing in the yard. I only did those things because my father and mother, as well as whoever watched my sister and me, believed that children belong outside playing and not stuck in the house watching television, playing video games, or getting in grown folks business. I, however, preferred writing in my journal. I had a vigilant imagination and very detailed dreams, so I always kept a pen or pencil and pad on me everywhere that I went. My peers perceived me as the strange, quiet kid who always wrote in her notepad. I even won an author's award in the second grade for a short story I wrote.

The detailed dreams I used to have showed me things about my future. How I would be different from my family and even how some of my loved ones didn't have my best interest at heart. It wasn't that they intentionally meant to harm me, it was just that they mostly thought of themselves first. They were self-centered. I can still remember, very clearly today, of a reoccurring dream I used to have. In this dream I was standing outside in my grandfather's yard helping him rake leaves into a large, deep, dark hole in the ground, and a family member (whose name I choose not to mention) pushed me into this hole. For months straight I had this dream, and I learned even then, at a young age, that I have to be careful and watchful of my surroundings, especially blood relatives.

Just as God spoke in Jeremiah 1:5, "Before I formed thee in the belly I knew thee; and before thou camest forth out of the womb I sanctified thee, and I ordained thee a prophet unto the nations," I strongly believe that God begins to prepare us for our purpose at a young age, as a child, as an infant in our parent's arms, as an embryo in the womb.

At the age of five, I was involved in a drive by shooting. Imagine how I felt from the age of five to fourteen after constantly being told that I should never have been born or, on any given day, being told that I should not have woken up that particular morning. From the age of seven through my high school years I would become very ill at sporadic times. A rash spread all over my face. My mother took me to several doctors, and I had to undergo many tests, but the doctors couldn't find anything wrong; this lasted for about a year. In middle school I started having muscle spasms in my shoulders and joint problems, which kept both my arms in arm slings. In high school I lost my vision at random moments for different periods of time, but the doctors said that my eyes were fine. Apparently I had twenty-twenty vision. Even while going through all of this with my physical body, I started teaching Sunday school to my age group when I was either 10 or 12-years-old. In those years I was learning that God was bigger then my ailments and problems.

I can't remember all the dreams that I had from the ages of 7 to 14-years-old, but I do remember many of them involved me running or flying away from people who were trying to harm me. However, when I turned 16-years-old, close to the end of my tenth grade year, I started having dreams that one of my parents was going to die before I would graduate from high school. Every time I had a dream like that, I woke up crying. The "death" dream persisted for two months until one night it was shown to me that my father was the parent who was going to die. Because my parents were never married, I often visited my father on the weekends. But after that revealing dream, I spent each and every weekend with my father during the three months leading up to his death. And from that point on I started taking my dreams seriously.

I was a quiet child, so I never told my family or my pastor the dreams I used to have. Until almost a year later I started having dreams about my mother dying. After having two of those discomforting dreams, I approached my pastor after service one Sunday and I began telling him of all the dreams that I had had in the past year and how they had all came true. More important, I told him I was afraid for my mother. After hearing this, and perhaps after recognizing my sincerity, he called the First Lady, deacons and mothers of the church over (with my mother), and we all began to pray for her. At that moment I began to understand that I was (and am) a dreamer. To this very day, I struggle with some of the things God shows me, has me to feel, even when I am not dreaming (sleep). This "gift" was something that I had to grow to accept.

During my earlier years, around the ages of 10 through 12, I knew that I had some type of calling on my life, but I never knew who I could talk to about it. There was definitely no one in my family whom I felt comfortable sharing this information with, so I kept it to myself. Then I went to college. While at Florida State University I thought, at first, that I could do what I wanted – forget about this calling thing and enjoy my college experience. Well, that barely lasted a year. I actually think I owe this to my roommate at the time. She would line up her teddy bears on her bed and have Bible study with them. Now, someone from the outside peeking in would think this to be strange behavior, but I one day walked in her room when I saw her reading to them and simply joined in. From that day forward, we started having Bible studies together. I started sharing with her the dreams that I would have, and she encouraged me to write them down. And together we watched them all manifest.

Later, we had friends who would come over to our Bible studies. These Bible studies kept growing. At one juncture, almost 14 people were gathered in our apartment every week. In addition to reading and studying the Word, we would have praise and worship and deliverance service. We even fasted on Wednesdays together. There was another group of about 20 college students who met up every Friday who heard about me on campus and looked me up. One day, my roommate and a friend came over and told me that the other group of college students had invited me to their studies. For almost two months, the amalgamated groups got together on Wednesdays and Fridays. Mind you, I had yet to accept my call. It was not until one high-spirited Friday night I started prophesying and laying hands on people that I knew, without a doubt, that I needed to stop running and accept my call to preach, to teach and to prophesy at the age of 20. When I accepted my call, God let me know that I was to be a true example of a minster of the gospel. Later on it was made clear unto me that I was to be a watchman. (For your edification, I implore you to read Ezekiel 3:16-27; 33:1-9.)

~~~

Everyone goes through something different when God begins to tug on them and reveal to them that they have a ministry calling on their life. Some people might accept their calling right away, while others may be like me and run from it, or put it on hold while they experience life. Or it could be even simpler. Maybe they don't (or didn't) have anyone with whom they can (or could) trust to discuss their being called. One thing I learned about God is that He does not silence the calling, and if you continue to drag your feet and run in the opposite direction, He will thrust you into His will. I seriously believe that I was not an example of a Christian. At least I don't think I was the Christian I should have been. But God called me anyway, and I had to shape my life up with the quickness because He had me on a fast-paced course making up for lost time.

Has God been tugging at you? At your heart? Have you realized that there is a calling on your life? If you are still questioning your call, please pray for clarity. If you are still running, stop. Accept your call today. Whether you believe it or not, someone desperately needs you. On the other hand, if you think you don't have a calling on your life, than you can be no more far from the truth. Understand that everyone has a calling. Callings vary in types and degrees, just as ministries and ministers vary in all type ethnicities, sizes, ages, and wisdom. Furthermore, all callings are needed to help the other. Ephesians 4:11-12 reads, "And he gave some, apostles; and some, prophets; and some, evangelists; and some, pastors and teachers; For the perfecting of the saints, for the work of the ministry, for the edifying of the body of Christ." Romans 12:3-5 reads, "For I say, through the grace given unto me, to every man that is among you, not to think of himself more highly than he ought to think; but to think soberly, according as God hath dealt to every man the measure of faith. For as we have many members in one body, and all members have not the same office: So we, being many, are one body in Christ, and every one members one of another."

When did you know you were called?

What are you called to do?

Are you walking in what you are called to do?

Chapter 2

"And as he journeyed, he came near Damascus: and suddenly there shined round about him a light from heaven: And he fell to the earth, and heard a voice saying unto him, Saul, Saul, why persecutest thou me? And he said, Who art thou, Lord? And the Lord said, I am Jesus whom thou persecutest: it is hard for thee to kick against the pricks. And he trembling and astonished said, Lord, what wilt thou have me to do? And the Lord said unto him, Arise, and go into the city, and it shall be told thee what thou must do. And the men which journeyed with him stood speechless, hearing a voice, but seeing no man. And Saul arose from the earth; and when his eyes were opened, he saw no man: but they led him by the hand, and brought him into Damascus. And he was three days without sight, and neither did eat nor drink...And Ananias went his way, and entered into the house; and putting his hands on him said, Brother Saul, the Lord, even Jesus, that appeared unto thee in the way as thou camest, hath sent me, that thou mightest receive thy sight, and be filled with the Holy Ghost. And immediately there fell from his eyes as it had been scales: and he received sight forthwith, and arose, and was baptized. And when he had received meat, he was strengthened. Then was Saul certain days with the disciples which were at Damascus. And straightway he preached Christ in the synagogues, that he is the Son of God."

-Acts 9:3-9; 17-20

Chapter 2: When Your Life Changes

Saul was a persecutor of the church. He was a man who tried to eliminate the church and rid the cities of the Christian presence. In the early verses of the ninth chapter of Acts, Saul shifts his focus from Jerusalem to Damascus (Acts 9:1-19). As Saul, with some of his attendants, traveled down a road to Damascus he experienced an account with the risen Jesus Christ. Acts 9:3 reads, "And as he journeyed, he came near Damascus: and suddenly there shined round about him a light from heaven." Saul, after falling to the earth, heard the voice of Christ asking him why he persecutes Him. Mind you, Saul was not a stranger to imprisoning the saints (Acts 8:3; 9:13). After Saul received directions from Christ, he rose to his feet, blinded, having to be led to Damascus by his attendants. For three whole days was Saul blinded and did not eat nor drink. One day while Ananias was praying God spoke to Ananias and had him to go to Saul and lay hands on him so that he would receive sight, as well as the Holy Ghost.

Acts 9:18 reads, "And immediately there fell from his eyes as it had been scales: and he had received sight forth with, and rose, and was baptized." As stated in chapter one (Accepting God's Purpose), sometimes God has to thrust you into His will because we sometimes go so far in the wrong direction that He has to take drastic, almost catastrophic, measures to get our attention. The sudden "thrust" is intended, necessary even, for us to experience him on a more personal level and to get us to do what He has purposed for us to do. When God spoke to Saul on the road to Damascus, none of the attendants heard the voice of Christ. Only Saul heard. Saul, who was far away from the call God had on his life, one day watched after the coats of men who eagerly stoned Stephen, the first Christian martyr who was chosen by the apostles for the special "service of the tables" (Acts 6:1-8).

It was not until Saul's road-to-Damascus experience that he changed his focus from persecuting God to preaching Christ. Acts 9:20 reads, "And straightway he preached Christ in the synagogues, that he is the Son of God." The encounter Saul had with Jesus Christ changed Saul's life completely and in Acts 13, God changed his name to Paul.

~~~

Most, if not all, people have experienced something that made them want to change their life. As I have mentioned before, God had to do something drastic in order to get them, or another, or possibly you, to accept the purpose that He has for them, or for you. I wonder at times why it takes God doing something miraculous or tragic in order for us to believe in Him and what He has called us to do. Over the years I have learned, through talking with various individuals, that people actually expect to hear from God before they make a move and adhere to what they believe is the right thing to do. One person even said, "God himself has to come down, stand in my face and tell me himself before I will move." My question is always, to whatever the decision making problem is, if you constantly feel and believe that B is the right choice and not A, then why not choose B and see what the outcome will be?

When I realized that I was a dreamer I started testing my dreams. If I dreamed about a particular date and a corresponding outcome, I would write it on my calendar, tell my roommate, and we would wait and see if it would happen. And guess what? It always did. Whenever I had a dream about any particular person, I would write it down and share it with my roommate (sometimes I would hold back names if she knew the individual and depending on the degree of the dream). I lie not; it never failed that they would come to pass. While doing this testing of my dreams, I noticed that a lot of my dreams manifested within a couple months, or even a couple hours.

You may be asking, "Well what does this have to do with your life changing?" Well, as I stated before, I was always a dreamer but it wasn't until I accepted my call from God that my dreams became deeper, more meaningful to me, and more relevant to others. Literally, whenever I dreamed I woke up feeling the emotions of my dreams. Whether happy, depressed, ashamed, or lost, I used to wake up with it all. I remember when I had a couple of dreams about people being in abusive relationships. Pain is all I felt for hours. I felt pain in the areas where, in my dreams, I saw people being abused on their body. A selected few individuals whom I told of these experiences told me that I had to pray for the abused souls because I was experiencing (feeling) what they felt. I also started having dreams about corrupt pastors, deceiving people, persons living double lives, those who practiced witchcraft and more. And because of this, I had to pray more, talk with God more and stay in His word forevermore. Because I had accepted what God had for me, my life had to change. I had to guard myself, my mind, my heart and soul; I had to change my circle of friends. Down to the very television shows I used to enjoy watching, they, too, had to change. It had gotten to the point that for almost two years I didn't watch television in my house unless it was a PG-13 movie that I had. Anything scary or demonic I did not watch. My whole demeanor changed because I was experiencing so much and it wasn't as simple as turning the gift off like flipping a light-switch. Whenever I wanted a so-called "break" (as if there is such a thing), especially when I wanted to sleep peacefully, I simply had to bite the bullet. There's no rest for the weary.

~~~

When you accept God's purpose for your life, your life will

change. It has to. At the moment of acceptance God begins to prepare you and show you things about yourself that you never knew about. You will notice, without your even trying, that your networks and friends will change, your eating habit may change, the conversations that you entertain will change, the way you dress and carry yourself may change, as well as your overall attitude. When a person seriously stops running from the call and grabs hold to God and His purpose, a breaking takes place. Breaking is necessary in order for God to remold you, remake you, sculpt you and design you to handle all that comes with your purpose. The bottom line is, your life has to change. However, the whole life-change aspect of accepting a call is difficult for many believers at first pass because who really wants to change when they are having fun, enjoying their friends, and doing what they like? Honestly, no one does! But change comes with life and with God's purpose for you. A purging is mandatory. Inescapable. Perhaps the change, transition wouldn't seem like a nightmare once believers realize that things have to be taken away in order for there to be room for what God wants to put in. Mess has to go and righteousness has to reign in your life.

Of course stepping out of your daily or weekly routine will cause problems at first, but you will eventually get used to it. It is sort of like choosing to eat healthier and sticking to that decision to eat healthier. Yes, the first 5 or 8 days may seem a breeze, but what about when the ninth day comes? When it seems like everything you can't eat, all of a sudden your mind and body craves? Hear me when I say that if you can press forward through the next three days and stay strong, you will start to think "oh, I can do this." Change can be difficult; you must pace yourself and stay positive.

Once you accept what God has for you and you make yourself fully available to Him, asking him to use you and letting Him know that His will is what you want for your life, God will begin to show you more of what's in you. Things that you never knew. At first, I simply thought that I was a dreamer. Then He started to give me visions, and then He gave me another gift, and another gift after that. Afterwhile, I realized that with every gift God gave, and will give, me, you, or anyone else, tests will follow and change will come. These are inevitable. Because God has to see how true you are to your calling.

Have you accepted God's purpose for your life?

Has your life changed in any way since you started walking in your calling?

How does change make you feel?

Chapter 3

"My brethren, count it all joy when ye fall into divers temptations; Knowing this, that the trying of your faith worketh patience."
-James 1:2-3

Chapter 3: Facing Unexpected Trials

Trials are the act or process of testing and trying by use and experience. Tests of patience or endurance. Trials are used during a test or tests. Trials have no respect of persons. They aren't bias nor prejudice. Trials show up in everyone's life. And everyone experiences and reacts to a trial differently. The Bible actually states that we should react to a trial or test with "joy" (James 1:2). So, how many of us really respond that way to a trial? The most simple answer is not many at all. When we look at a trial or even hear the mention of the word, we affix a negative connotation to the word. We think of loss, pain, burden, struggle, restlessness, suffering and any other seemingly negative, pessimistic word. God, however, looks at this word differently than we do. He looks at is a process to test our will, patience, endurance and dedication. He uses trials to guide us and help us rid ourselves of dead weight and things that are not needed. These trials are sent to purge us and test our inner selves, our character. To find out what's in our hearts and show us our worth to Him and the kingdom. During these trials we really learn who we are and how much we can take. If God never test us or push us to, what we presume to be, our limits, then we will never know how strong we really are. We will never move to the next level because we constantly tell ourselves "I can't handle that." In God's word he reassures us that He will not put more on us than we can bear. So if we find ourselves in a trial, then obviously we can bare it.

There are various trials. Trials that test our faith, finances, patience, character, strength, family, obedience, motives and so much more. When a trial comes you can't quit, get depressed, or become frustrated. You have to know that God is positioning you for your purpose and that each trial is something you have to go through. Once you say "yes" to God, you will encounter many trials. It's not because you are in trouble. And it's not because God wants to punish you. It is because you have to learn who you are and what your worth is to the kingdom; God has to see if you are willing to suffer just as He had to suffer. The Bible reads in II Timothy 2:11-13, "It is a faithful saying: For if we be dead with him, we shall also live with him: If we suffer, we shall also reign with him: if we deny him, he also will deny us: If we believe not, yet he abideth faithful: he cannot deny himself." Trials and suffering will come but tied to them is life and reigning with Christ.

~~~

When I accepted my purpose at first it seemed that my life was still the same. I was ending my sophomore year at Florida State University, I was the president of two major organizations on campus, I had great friends and I really didn't have too many troubles, until people started to notice my change of character and how I didn't want to be in certain environments nor entertain certain conversations. Needless to say friends started dropping quickly. I even noticed that my patience for excuses and worldly compromises had left. I no longer dealt with foolishness because I realized that I had wasted a lot of time when I was running from my call. I had ended a three year relationship, and no less than a month later, I found myself in yet another relationship with someone else. The difference in the two is that this young man was a minister and since I had just accepted my call three months prior, I thought that this would be a great relationship. I was still in school, I had everything I asked for, I had my own car, apartment; everything seemed to be great. I became the collegiate ministry coordinator at church, I joined the mime ministry and even helped on the hospitality ministry at my, then, boyfriend's church. Can you see how or why I thought everything was good? Well, a few months into my great relationship, I started noticing some things that were wrong to me.

I always held onto a misconception that every godly relationship, especially between ministers, was a strong one. Since they both love God, pray, read the word, live an honest Christian life and so forth, I thought a relationship like the one I was in would prove to be a wonderful example of a couple being equally yoked. Was I wrong? Yes. I was. This mini trial blew my mind. Since we both were members of separate ministries, I never thought that he or I would become jealous of the other or ask for the other to change. The day I gave my initial sermon he chose not to come. When I invited him to early morning services at my church, an excuse was always given. He knew my family was coming into town to visit with me, but he made other arrangements. When meetings were made for him and me to commune with my former pastor, he would back out. I must have went through this for about a year. I had started to feel like I would have been better off remaining in my last relationship. Mind you, the only reason why I ended my previous relationship. We were "unequally yoked." To this very day, I still don't understand why when his church had a function, I was there, or when he wanted me to meet his pastor and family, I did. I even drove out of town to meet his family and network of friends on many occasions. When it hit me that I supported him more than he supported me I purposely arranged for us to meet one afternoon to end the relationship. I just could not believe that Christian relationships went through simple troubles as those. Really, what's the problem with supporting each other and our ministries? After that relationship, I decided that it would be only me and God for a while. I really believe that that's why that relationship had so many issues; because I wasn't single long enough. I was probably single for every bit of two weeks and I'm sure I brought some issues to the relationship; he just never made me aware of them.

When it became just me and God He put me through test after test after test. Even while writing this book, I am going through a major test, which I discuss in detail in "When All Is Lost." It seemed that there were always misunderstanding, loneliness and confusion going on. Even though I became more active in the church, made the moves I knew God told me to make, moved to the other side of town to live alone with no roommate, graduated from college and started working my first job. On the outside, everything appeared to be great. Only my closest friends knew that I was going through much within myself. Yet, despite my personal situations, I kept mentoring people; helping people financially; doing group sessions and Bible studies in my apartment; going around town praying for people, their roommates and residence; making sure people had food to eat or a ride to get to their next destination. I was helping whoever needed a place to stay, providing understanding to those who were confused and yet I was being broken all the while. Still having dreams, still having visions, learning that I had the gift of prophecy, healing and discernment was not helping me help myself deal with me being broken because God put in me a great amount of compassion for His people. So it seemed that I couldn't help myself because I was too busy helping others. So I learned - ministry doesn't stop when God is making you over. At least He didn't allow me to sit on the side line or ride the bench while I was undergoing spiritual corrective surgery.

~~~

Everyone goes through different unexpected trials. Mine may not seem as serious as yours, but to me mine leave me wondering "why am I experiencing this?" If you don't mind, let us spend the next part of this chapter dissecting three types of trials.

Trial of Faith

This is a trial that challenges us to suppress our own plans and desires to take matters into our own hands. In faith we must fully submit our timetable and expectations to the will of God. When you said yes to God and accepted the purpose and destiny He has for you, a trial of faith has, or will indubitably come your way. To have faith is to believe in what is not presently before you but promised to you in the future. Believing in what is not seen and living on the hope of what's to come. Therefore with every promise there is a test. Abraham and Sarah received precise promises from God. One well known, almost to the point of cliché, is the promise of a son in their old age even though Sarah was technically barren (Genesis 15:4). Years pass and the promise wasn't fulfilled yet so they took matters into their own hands and made a mess of things. A house was divided and God's promise still wasn't manifested. Maybe Abraham and Sarah's lack of faith delayed their promise from coming to fruition. This test of faith lasted for almost 25 years. However, in research, archaeologist discovered ancient tablets that contained marriage contracts specifying that a barren woman was required to provide a woman for her husband for the purpose of procreation. This was an acceptable cultural practice, back then, to handle what they thought could not be changed.

Abraham was called by God in Genesis 12; Abraham left his country because God told him to do so. God didn't even tell him where he would be going but Abram (as he was called before God changed his name) packed up his things and moved. Since he left the familiar for the unfamiliar, how could he not have faith in God when God promised him a child? Abraham had allowed thought patterns and practices that he had learned from his pagan culture to influence his thinking. Which shows us that we have to go through tests and trials to get rid of our old thought patterns and beliefs. If we have faith in God we have to show it and live it at all times no matter what trials we may face. Romans 14:23 states that "whatever is not from faith is sin."

Trial of Inconsistency

When you go through this trial, things don't go the way you think that they should. During this type of trial, you have to trust God when things seem inconsistent and contradictory to His word. God sends inconsistencies to test our reaction and responses. Will we become broken or bitter? Soft or hard? In the year 2007 I wrote a blog on my Myspace page titled "Question" and an excerpt from it reads, "Knowing what your destiny is and seeing what God is calling you to do gives you a better understanding of what and why you are going through what you are going through. You will see that God is truly preparing you through your trials, mind battles, sleepless nights, bedside prayers and fountains of tears for a better future; for your destiny. Yes your situation may contradict the God that you serve because you know Him as a healer, a provider, a peace maker, a way maker and so much more. But what do you do when your situation contradicts who He is?"

A writer penned, "For out of my emptiness others had been blessed with fruitfulness. Out of my brokenness others received wholeness. Out of my weakness other had received strength. Slowly but surely, this spiritual law of contradiction that had been in the shadows of obscurity was beginning to take on clarity."

In scripture we find Joseph; a dreamer. Joseph dreamed of promotion and prosperity but was thrown into a pit by his brothers. Later, Joseph was sold into Egypt, then imprisoned on false accusations. Joseph experienced many acts of hatred before he was promoted to the palace as the administrator of Egypt. What if Joseph would have quit on his dream?

When you accepted Jesus as your personal Savior, and your response was yes to your purpose, you agreed to bear your cross (Matthew 16:24) and in carrying your cross you are destined to experience some inconsistencies. Hebrews

12:2-3 reads, "Looking unto Jesus the author and finisher of our faith; who for the joy that was set before him endured the cross, despising the shame, and is set down at the right hand of the throne of God. For consider him that endured such contradiction of sinners against himself, lest ye be wearied and faint in your minds." If God had to experience it, so do you. What would or could give you the inclination that you're exempt from hardship?

During the trial of inconsistencies are you able to confess "as for God, His way is perfect; the word of the Lord is proven" (Psalm 18:30)?

Trial of Character

Trials of character address your true personality. To see if you will fall under pressure and lash out at God and others. These trials are designed to see if you are truly a Christian who is devoted to God. These trials test your faith in order to see if it is fake and to see if your outer appearance is a façade. God wants to test your character to make sure it is right for your purpose.

Lets quickly look at the story of Hannah, which means grace, graciousness or favor. Hannah was a barren woman married to Elkanah who had another wife named Peninnah who had given him sons and daughters. Hannah desperately wanted a child, specifically a man-child, to receive the inheritance of Elkanah. Every year the family would take a journey to make a sacrifice and celebrate the blessings of

God on their home. But Hannah really didn't have much to celebrate, especially when all Peninnah's children were being blessed and celebrated (I Samuel 1:3-6). Instead of Hannah making a scene, shouting, murmuring and walking around with an attitude, she simply found herself a place where she could pray and talk to God. Yes, I Samuel 1:10 says "she was in bitterness of soul," but that didn't stop her from interceding for herself (I Samuel 1:11-19). She spoke from her heart and poured out her soul before the Lord. She didn't allow her trial of character, her inability to bare a child, affect her negatively. As a matter of fact, her trial pushed her closer to God. Her character changed not, she remained gracious and she bore Samuel, the great and wise prophet-judge.

What trials are you facing?

How are you handling the tests God brings your way?

Through your trials was there a positive change in your character? How so?

Chapter 4

"Wherefore take unto you the whole armour of God, that ye may be able to withstand in the evil day, and having done all, to stand. Stand therefore, having your loins girt about with truth, and having on the breastplate of righteousness; And your feet shod with the preparation of the gospel of peace; Above all, taking the shield of faith, wherewith ye shall be able to quench all the fiery darts of the wicked. And take the helmet of salvation, and the sword of the Spirit, which is the word of God"

-Ephesians 6:13-17

Chapter 4: Mind Control

One of the most important things to have, especially when life throws you an awkward hand, is mind control. When trials come and your life becomes disheveled and you don't know what to do or you can't make sense of why you are experiencing road blocks, failed tries and constant confusion, you have to have mind control. It's not an option. A lot of people fail and quit and fall by the way side because they cannot control their thoughts. They let their emotions get the best of them. Ephesians 6:13 reads, "Wherefore take unto you the whole armor of God, that ye may be able to withstand in the evil day, and having done all, to stand." The part of this armor that I want to focus on is the "helmet of salvation" (v. 17).

The helmet worn in battles was a cap made of thick leather, or brass, fitted to the head, and was usually crowned with a plume, or crest, as an ornament. Its use was to guard the head from a blow by a sword, war-club, or battle-axe. So the hope of conquering every adversary and surmounting every difficulty, through the blood of Christ, is a helmet that protects the head; an impenetrable one, that the blow of the battle-axe cannot cleave. The helmet defended the heads of the soldiers who went to battle. The head is a vital part of the body. So to have a helmet of salvation, which is to have the hope of salvation, defends the soul and keeps it from the blows of the enemy. The hope of continual safety and protection, which is built on the promises of God, to which the upright follower of Christ feels he has a Divine right, protects the understanding from being darkened, and the judgment from being confused by any temptations of Satan, or subtle arguments of the sophistical ungodly. For he who carries Christ in his heart cannot be cheated out of the hope of his heaven. Also, a soldier would not fight without a hope of victory.

If you do some research and look for a picture of a Grecian helmet from the Fifth Century, B.C., you will notice that the helmet has a large ornament on it designed to guard blows. Not only that, the helmet protects the entire head. It is very unlike a bicycle helmet. When Christians wear the helmet of salvation, Satan has to work hard at attacking their minds. And if the individual falls into temptation, it is because he or she wanted to. When God controls your mind, Satan cannot lead you astray.

I Thessalonians 5:8 reads, "But let us, who are of the day, be sober, putting on the breastplate of faith and love; and for an helmet, the hope of salvation."

The head of a soldier was among the principal parts to be defended, as on it the deadliest strokes might fall, and it is the head that controls the whole body. The head is the seat of the mind, which, when it has laid hold of the sure Gospel "hope" of eternal life, will not receive false doctrine, or give way to Satan's temptations. We should not allow despair, depression and doubt to enter into our mind when we have the "hope of salvation." This means that all was paid on the cross. When you received Christ as your personal Lord and Savior, you started gaining greater knowledge of who He is, while also building a relationship with Him. That being said, it should not be easy for you to lose your mind.

~~~

What is the mind? The mind is the consciousness that originates in the brain and directs mental and physical behavior. The mind is a chest that holds memory, recollection, conscious thoughts, attention, opinion and or intentions, as well as intellect and intelligence. So if you allow Satan to get into your mind you can become mindless, walking around lacking intelligence, sense, or purpose. You become careless and heedless, making the wrong choices and doing things that you would not normally do. You begin to change your language, desires and your attention is then turned into the wrong direction. At all times you should have on your helmet of salvation because the devil comes to tempt you, play with your mind, and cause you to lose focus. If ever you take your helmet off, you give the devil room for attack, and, in turn, you kill your own purpose, aimlessly living your life, never reaching your full potential.

Romans 5:1-5 reads, "Therefore being justified by faith, we have peace with God through our Lord Jesus Christ: By whom also we have access by faith into this grace wherein we stand, and rejoice in hope of the glory of God. And not only so, but we glory in tribulations also: knowing that tribulation worketh patience; And patience, experience; and experience, hope: And hope maketh not ashamed; because the love of God is shed abroad in our hearts by the Holy Ghost which is given unto us."

We get better at mind control through experience. Through experience hope is increased and with the hope of salvation we are strengthened to fight off the mind wars of Satan. You have to begin to look at your situations differently. You can't allow yourself to get depressed when things don't go your way or when you simply don't understand the fight. If you have the mind of Christ, and if you walk with a renewed mind, not being double-minded, your life will have more peace, joy and control in it.

When I experience hardship, when trials come, when the unexpected happens, I've learned to shift my thinking and look at my problems differently. I begin to ask God, "What is the purpose behind this test?" because I've learned that we all go through hardship for a reason. Whether it is to purge us, change us, equip us, or to learn something about God, about our relationship with God, or about ourselves. You can sing that God is your provider, your healer, and your peace, but when you experience a test and come with your hands lifted up in victory, there will be no doubt in your mind who God is to you. No one can make you doubt Him; Satan can't tempt you because you have experienced who God is for yourself. For Romans 14: 5 tells us, "Let every man be fully persuaded in his own mind." Once you put it in your mind that you are going to live the purpose that God has for you, nothing and no one can stop you but yourself.

I can remember when I was 16 years old, in the eleventh grade, my father had passed. To me, that was one of the worst things that could have ever happened to me in life. A daddy's girl I was to the core and I always got what I wanted. My father always made sure I didn't lack anything. I used to love laying under him because there was peace when I was in his presence. Major cares? I had none. I only cared about spending time with him. In my father's house the windows in the dinning room and front living room were oversized. The front living room was actually our favorite spot in the house. It had no television and no phone; it was simply decorated with family pictures, a sofa, a love seat, a sofa chair, a center table and two end tables. We used to lie on a couch and look out the window while talking. He usually fell asleep before I did, but I didn't mind because that was my daddy, and spending time with him is all I cared about. I always enjoyed those quiet, peaceful moments together.

When I woke up on November 7, 2000, I received the news of my father's death. To me, it seemed as though my world had ended. I walked around my house depressed. I would leave school and have someone drop me off at my dad's house just so I could lay on the sofa in our favorite room. I must have laid on that sofa for almost two weeks until family and friends said that I could no longer lie in the room like that. I hadn't noticed at the time, but I stopped eating. One day, an acquaintance of my dad's family told me that I was slowly killing myself due to depression.

Along with my dad's death and dealing with personal issues that I had with my mother, I began to develop this "I don't care" attitude. I didn't care if I died or lived nor did I care about anyone else's feelings because I was hurting and no one could help me because they all had their own issues.

When I finally got fed up with my living arrangements, I lived with various people at various places until I graduated from high school and moved to Tallahassee to attend Florida State University.

Before I left Plant City, I was living two lives from the time of my daddy's death until I left town. I would still go to church, teach Sunday school, and sit on the same third pew every Sunday as if everything was okay, as if nothing had changed. I would go to school, pass my classes and leave. I was only going through the motions. What I wanted, or at least what I thought I wanted, at the time was just to die. I started listening to the temptations of Satan, as he spoke through my family and friends. At the age of 16 I started drinking and going to clubs. I can remember an uncle and cousins of mine who gave me liquor to drink when I lived with my mother. So when I moved from under my mother's roof, I found friends who would buy me the liquor and next thing I know, I was taking liquor to school. I was drinking probably three days out of the week just to suppress my emotions. I went through the different levels of depression alone. I remember being depressed for 18 months because it seemed that no one cared.

In the early months of 2002, I had a life changing experience so I stopped drinking. I seriously started to hear, "your daddy's death can no longer be your excuse." His death was really the reason why I accepted the first cup of alcoholic beverage and that was because he was no longer there and I held on tight to the "I don't care" mentality. It wasn't until I moved to Tallahassee, in June of 2002, that I started really dealing with my father's death. I stopped drinking, but I ended up going back through the levels of depression because the first time around I didn't deal with his death the right way. I stopped eating all over again. I got extremely sick for almost eight months and for a short while I was put on medication. If it had not been for my roommate, and two other friends, there's no telling where I (or my mind) would be. My mother used to drive to Tallahassee from Plant City every two months to check-up on me.

Levels of Depression

1. Shock and Denial

2. Pain and Guilt

3. Anger and Bargaining

4. Sadness, Reflection, Loneliness

5. The Upward Turn

6. Reconstruction and Working Through

7. Acceptance and Hope

The crazy thing about this experience is that I learned even though I always went to church (I got saved in 1995 and baptized in 1996), paid my tithes, read the Bible, listened to gospel music and got involved, that I was heading straight to hell. I realized that doing all those things didn't matter because my heart wasn't right, my motives were wrong, and my mind was stuck in a routine.

I had to slow down, pause and take myself back through the basics of being a Christian. It was just me and God (and of course my roommate) because I had issues with preachers.

From this very experience I learned how to control my

thought patterns. I never again wanted another tragedy, trial or test to affect me the way my father's death had. So, now when I go through, I simply think, "there must be a reason" for every trial and test I encounter and move on. Because I made a promise to myself that I will never again break down nor lose my mind.

II Timothy 1: 7, "For God hath not given us the spirit of fear; but of power, and of love, and of a sound mind."

Have you ever had to change the way you thought about a trial?

Are you willing to think positively about future trials? Will you be able to view them as stepping stones, each step taking you higher and closer to your purpose?

What causes you to struggle with controlling your thoughts (mind)?

Chapter 5

"The glory of this latter house shall be greater than of the former, saith the LORD of hosts: and in this place will I give peace, saith the LORD of hosts."

-Haggai 2:9

Chapter 5: When All Is Lost

When it appeared that everything was back on track in my life, God started making some adjustments all over again. In March of 2008, I was about to get my second promotion on my job until He told me to deny the offer because He was about to move me. I began to question God and ask Him where I was going. The answer He gave made me feel as though God had really lost His mind and missed the mark. He had told me that I was moving back home and that was something I dreaded. Once I got out of Plant City, I never had the urge to return. I never got homesick and I rarely made visits. So when God said that He was moving me and that I had to go back home, I only listened to the first part of His word and I began to aid Him, or so I thought, in looking for me a job out of the state of Florida. I even started looking for places to live in California, Texas, Virginia, New York, Washington D.C. and a few other states, but a job never came through. I did do as He said, however, and denied the offer of the promotion. I had told my supervisors that I was moving soon and that it appeared that I was moving back home.

Once I accepted God's choice I started to make frequent visits to Hillsborough County for interviews and apartment searching. When nothing immediately came through from either search, I thought that I had missed the mark, that I had misunderstood God's word. But I had later got a call from my mother stating that I can move my belongings into one of my grandfather's houses and even live in it. Finally, it seemed that things were starting to change for the better. Well, my lease in Tallahassee didn't end till the end of June, so I continued to work and saved money for the big move back home. All of a sudden, in the month of April, 2008, I got sick. In May I had to undergo surgery for the first time. This was a crazy, nervous experience because I kept wondering "what if the doctors do something wrong?" or "what if I die?" I later found out that I actually did stop breathing a couple of times after they moved me to the recovery room. Because of the type of surgery that I had, I couldn't drive, let alone leave the house, for two weeks. When I tried to return to work, the staples the doctor put in me started to rip through my flesh so I had to resign from my position sooner than I thought. In the month of June, I probably went to work for a total of eight days.

I really thanked God during this time for my Sorority sisters and friends because they came by daily to see about me. My old roommate even moved in with me for a while and helped pack up some of my things because I was still scheduled to move out at the end of the month. Through this experience, God really humbled me because I wasn't, and never had been, the type of person who asked for help.

Typically, I was the one who always gave help. He turned the tables to teach me something, that I needed people. I had started to think that people needed me more than I needed them because I was well off and could do for myself. I also learned to value life because I came close to losing it a couple of times on that hospital bed. While I was still recuperating from the surgery, I moved back to Plant City. Upon arrival, I quickly learned that my "storage house" needed many small repairs so I couldn't live in it right away. All I could do at the time was leave my belongings there and move in with one of my older sisters. Living there was shady because I didn't know when my sister would want me to move out and if I would be living somewhere else the next day. Because I didn't want to wear out my welcome at my sister's, I would intentionally find ways and reasons to get back to Tallahassee and spend a few nights with some old friends for a few days out of each month. Eventually, my welcome did run out, or at least wore very thin. Actually, my sister had asked me to move out on three separate occasions, but she allowed me to stay with her for almost a year.

When I moved back to my hometown, I watched after my grandfather five days out of the week from either 7:00 a.m. or 9:00 a.m. to 5:00 p.m. for almost six months until other family members were asked to watch after him, for which they were paid a nominal fee. All the while I was going on interview after interview. I started to hear the same thing over and over; employers kept telling me I was over qualified. Until then, I thought that phrase was only said on television shows and in movies. But this was real life, my life. I applied to over 250 jobs in one year and 75% of them said the same thing, "You are over qualified". Jobs that used to require a college degree now only asked that applicants have a high school diploma or G.E.D. Since I didn't have bills - my mother paid my cell phone bill and car insurance - I didn't get frustrated about the situation until I over heard my mother saying that she hoped I didn't get a job. I understood that she didn't mean to say this to hurt me; she said it because she was concerned about someone being available to help keep and stay with her father during the day while she worked, which I didn't mind doing voluntarily because he is my grandfather and because he did step in to help financially when my father passed. But because I didn't have a paying job, I had to go some days without eating. In addition, I didn't have a place of my own, I started feeling like people were using me, and it was all a bit overwhelming.

The people I volunteered to help in various places talked about me behind my back. People would tell me on more than one occasion or another that they would hire me for a particular position, but their words only sounded good. They never hired me, and perhaps they never intended to hire me. After a while, my savings ran out and during this year of financial instability, thieves broke into my storage house and stole some of my belongings. Shortly afterwards, my family members started revealing some of their corruptive and deceitful ways. In the end, I had to move my furniture and other items from my storage house to a regular storage unit. And in a matter of two weeks, I had to move out of my sister's house. It looked like I was going to become homeless.

So what did I do? I left town and went back to the place where I knew I could depend on people. I went back to Tallahassee. I only went back for a few days, but only because God kept telling me that I couldn't leave. At this juncture in my life I had lost it all. Still, I couldn't really understand how God could have me to move back home where family lived to lose all that I had worked so hard for.

After my two-day retreat, I returned to Hillsborough County. I withdrew all the money in my CD (Certified Deposit) so that I could move all my items from the storage house into a commercial storage facility until I found a place to live. A month later, I found an apartment and used whatever monies I had left to move in. However, I noticed that my furniture that I only had for barely two years was ruined, damaged terribly, as well as my mattresses. I was devastated. I had left Tallahassee with enough furniture to furnish a fairly large-sized apartment. A year later I only had a bookshelf and an empty entertainment stand to display in my new apartment. And I still did not have a job.

I worked all summer at a youth camp, hoping to receive my check which would allow me to put furniture in my apartment. Did I receive anything when paychecks were cut? No. For the past three months or more, I have been sleeping, sitting, and eating on the floor. Even as I write this book I am laying on the floor. Still, I have no furniture but a friend from Tallahassee gave me a television. In a matter of 15 months, from the time I moved from Tallahassee back to Plant City, I slowly but surely lost everything. My trust in the words of men is lost, too. I no longer hold people to their word. Nowadays, people have to show me their word.

There have been a few times while dealing with this season that I'm in when I wanted to quit. I got like Elijah when he sat up under the juniper tree, "Lord just take my life." It took 13 months for me to truly get fed up with the hand I was dealt. I found myself relating to the Israelites in the wilderness. How can you take me from a place of plenty to put me in a place of lack? Just as God provided manna for the Israelites, He definitely provided for me, but His provision wasn't given in the way that I had wanted. Unlike the Israelites, I refused to complain, murmur and gripe because I know that I did answer God with a "yes." Even though I have lost it all, my answer is still "yes." I have learned from times past that God does things and allows things to happen for a reason. He obviously is preparing me for a higher calling, taking me somewhere major, somewhere I haven't been before. Why else would he allow for me to lose all that I had saved and worked hard for? As stated in the "Facing Unexpected Trials" chapter, I know that with every promise, there is a trial. And I know I did not, and am not, going through in vain because II Corinthians 1:20 reads, "For all the promises of God in him are yea, and in him Amen, unto the glory of God by us." It was verses like this that has kept my mind. When I said yes to my purpose, I also said yes to suffering for Christ's sake. In my losing everything, I learned more about who God is.

Have you ever experienced a lost?

What verses do you meditate on when you go through a season of losing?

How did you behave when God started to take things and people away? Did your character change? If so, how so?

Chapter 6

"And let us consider one another to provoke unto love and to good works: Not forsaking the assembling of ourselves together, as the manner of some is; but exhorting one another: and so much the more, as ye see the day approaching."

-Hebrews 10:24-25

Chapter 6: Environment is Key

Once you receive Christ as your personal Lord and Savior your environment has to change. There is no choice in the matter. God prefers for his children to be around like-minded people, individuals who are striving to better themselves in their Christian journey. People who have decided to die to the things of this world and live solely committed to God. When we place ourselves in environments that are godly we are then encouraged, uplifted and supported. Hebrews 10:25 encourages us to exhort one another, which means in godly types of environments we shouldn't be slandering one another, gossiping, or tearing each other down. Rather we should be telling our own personal testimony to give others strength to endure their trials, letting them know that if God did it for you then He can and will surely do the same for them.

When God has impregnated you with purpose, you have to actively be involved with what you allow to happen in your environment. You can't stand around and watch or allow anything (i.e. violence, gossip, sex related sins and et cetera) to happen in your environment. You can't simply sit around and listen to anything either. As I've heard many times before, "you have to guard your gates." You have to protect yourself. You cannot allow any old thing to enter into you, the Lord's tabernacle where the Spirit resides. You may be asking, "What are your gates?" They are your senses. What you see, hear, smell, taste or speak, and even touch.

While taking classes for an endorsement certificate for pre-kindergarten disabilities, I learned that what a mother puts in her body can affect the fetus and the baby, while in the womb. When pregnant women allow hazardous elements to enter their body, their babies can grow to be disabled, can be birthed prematurely and can even die in the womb. When God puts that purpose, vision or dream in you, you can't allow toxic elements to taint the purpose growing inside of you. What people may say or think is healthy may not be healthy for you and your calling. What's healthy in the carnal world to carnal people, may not exactly be healthy in the spiritual world or for spiritual purposes. Judges 13:13-14 reads, "And the angel of the LORD said unto Manoah, of all that I said unto the woman let her beware. She may not eat of any thing that cometh of the vine, neither let her drink wine or strong drink, nor eat any unclean thing: all that I commanded her let her observe." Once you are impregnated, what you may desire to eat, see or touch must be eluded because you now have to do what's in the best interest of your baby, your purpose. Your environment and daily routine has to change.

Acts 2:42 tells us, "And they continued stedfastly in the apostles' doctrine and fellowship, and in breaking of bread, and in prayers." While birthing the purpose that God has for you, you must fill your environment with people and things devoted to the apostle's doctrine, fellowship, breaking of bread, and prayers.

The Apostle's Doctrine: Teaching or instruction, particularly that of Jesus or the apostles concerning God's will. This will require you to spend more time in God's word, learning His will so that you may effectively live the will He has for your life. You have to attend services (i.e. Bible Study and Sunday Morning Worship) to be taught the truths of God. Colossians 1:25-28 reads, "Whereof I am made a minister, according to the dispensation of God which is given to me for you, to fulfill the word of God; Even the mystery which hath been hid from ages and from generations, but now is made manifest to his saints: To whom God would make known what is the riches of the glory of this mystery among the Gentiles; which is Christ in you, the hope of glory: Whom we preach, warning every man, and teaching every man in all wisdom; that we may present every man perfect in Christ Jesus."

Fellowship: Companionship; a group of persons with a common interest. Among Christians, the common bond is their faith in Jesus Christ. Your environment should include the fellowship of like-minded individuals. You will need to surround yourself with people who will encourage you to push when the time comes to push. Philippians 2:1-3 reads, "if there be therefore any consolation in Christ, if any comfort of love, if any fellowship of the Spirit, if any bowels and mercies, Fulfill ye my joy, that ye be likeminded, having the same love, being of one accord, of one mind. Let nothing be done through strife or vainglory;

but in lowliness of mind let each esteem [the] other better than themselves."

Breaking of Bread: One of the many forms of an intimate fellowship is breaking bread with one another. I'm not talking about having communion; I'm talking about eating one with another. A common event among college students, which I found out during my undergraduate years, is potlucks. Potlucks allow for individuals to get together and bring a covered dish. Whenever I attended such festivities, I noticed that people stayed around a little while longer and conversations lasted longer which were filled with various topics. There is something about people and food. And for someone to actually eat your food meant something because there are persons who don't eat just anybody's food. This type of fellowship allows you to be yourself. You usually don't have to dress in your Sunday's best, jeans and a t-shirt will do just fine. Matthew 15:34-37a reads, "And Jesus saith unto them, How many loaves have ye? And they said, Seven, and a few little fishes. And he commanded the multitude to sit down on the ground. And he took the seven loaves and the fishes, and gave thanks, and brake them, and gave to his disciples, and the disciples to the multitude. And they did all eat, and were filled." When I looked up the word "potluck" it was defined as: whatever food happens to be available for a meal, especially when offered to a guest.

Prayer: Words that are addressed to God. This should definitely be a part of your environment. Your house should become that of prayer. You should also find individuals whom you can pray with. In Matthew 21:22 the Lord states, "And all things, whatsoever ye shall ask in prayer, believing, ye shall receive." There are two components to prayer. First, you have to believe in what you are asking God for. Second, you have to be mindful of the people who you choose to pray with.

~~~

A lot of times with a person's purpose God sends them into the wilderness. The length of time spent in the wilderness usually depends on the individual and their purpose. The wilderness is usually the place of preparation for where God is taking you next. Most individuals are trained in the wilderness to be isolated and fully dependent upon God. Prophetic persons are usually thrown into the wilderness sooner than others, but all persons with a purpose have to experience some form of the wilderness. The training of Moses was in the wilderness. He was given the promise of freeing the Israelites from Egypt, but he was sent to the wilderness because he needed to be prepared for the promise. Elijah was told by God to go and hide by the brook Cherith. While there, he is fed by ravens and drank water from a brook (I Kings17:2-6). John the Baptist had to spend some time in the wilderness, too, before he could be a mouthpiece for Jesus Christ (Matthew 3:1-3). Before Jesus casted out demons, healed the sick, and operated in the power of the Holy Spirit, he was sent to the wilderness to be tempted, tested and tried by the devil (Matthew 4:1-11). Luke 4:13-14 reads, "And when the devil had ended all the temptation, he departed from him for a season. And Jesus returned in the power of the Spirit into Galilee: and there went out a fame of him through all the region round about."

In the wilderness environment a person learns a lot about self, personal strengths and weaknesses. Time in the wilderness should be devoted to God's teaching and preparation for who you are called to be in God's

Kingdom. The wilderness shouldn't be seen negatively, but it should be seen as a place of training, elevation and transformation.

Through my wilderness experience I can definitely say that I have learned myself. The experience pushed me into an environment, alone, isolated; it was just me and God. He removed me off my clutch, away from my support group in Tallahassee, and he intentionally made them too busy to hear most of my concerns, frustrations or to hear me when I wanted someone to vent to.

Is the company you keep conducive to your purpose?

What environment changes do you have to make?

Have you ever had a wilderness experience? If so, what was it like? What did you learn about your strengths and weaknesses? If not, are you prepared or preparing for the time you will spend in the wilderness?

Chapter 7

"Though he slay me, yet will I trust in him"

-Job 13:15

Chapter 7: Contractions

The word "contraction" can be defined as the shortening and thickening of a muscle for the purpose of exerting force or causing movement of a body part; a rhythmic tightening in labor of the upper uterine musculature that contracts the size of the uterus and pushes the fetus toward the birth canal. The experience of contractions varies from one person to the next. Contractions can also vary for the same person in different parts of the labor as well as from one labor to the next.

Almost all women experience lower abdominal pain during contractions. Lower back pains are also expected. Pains throughout the belly, hip and or thighs can be, and most likely are, felt. Pain can travel from front to back, back to front, or down the thighs. This pain can also happen all at once. Women who have actually experienced labor describe their pains as including: aching, cramping, pressing, throbbing, sharp and shooting. These pains usually intensify as labor progresses.

Through research, I ironically learned that the pushing phase of labor is less painful than the contractions. This means that the individual really must have mind control. Since contractions are known to come on a rhythmic pattern, they tire a person out; so when it is the right time to push, they often are too tired and fatigued to do so. This is why each woman needs a support team in the labor room; to encourage them to push. With every contraction the fetus is pushed to the birth canal, but it is the job of the woman, the mother, to push with every contraction once the fetus is in the right position.

When God puts the seed of purpose in you, as that seed grows into a fetus, your life then begins to change. You begin to face unexpected trials and, more than ever before, test after test starts to barrage your life. These tests (contractions) are being used to force your purpose in to place so that you can push your purpose out. Some people experience labor for days whereas others have delayed labor.

~~~

Women are not the only people whom God impregnates with purpose. Let's look at the life of Job. A man who went through contractions in order to fulfill the purpose God had for him. Job's purpose was to be the example of a man who can go through, lose it all, and still not curse God. He experienced trial after trial to learn God for himself as well as to teach his friends and family, who had the misconception that God does not test "good people." Job had to lose it all just to learn God, learn his own strengths, and teach everyone around him.

The book of Job was written by an unknown author during an unknown time to disclose of God's sovereignty. Job 13:15 reads, "Though he slay me, yet will I trust in him." One thing after the next started to go wrong for Job. He lost his oxen and donkeys, his servants were slain by the Sabeans, his sheep and servants were consumed in a fire, his camels were taken away and more servants were slain by the Chaldeans, and then his eldest son's house collapses and kills all his children (Job 1:13-19). With all this happening to Job, his response was, "Naked came I out of my mother's womb, and naked shall I return thither: the LORD gave, and the LORD hath taken away; blessed be the name of the LORD" (v.21). The writer then penned, "In all this Job sinned not, nor charged God foolishly" (v.22). Job was later afflicted to his body with "sore boils from the sole of his foot unto his crown" (Job 2.7). His wife even told him to curse God and die (v.9), but Job did no such thing.

It appears that the author of the book of Job wrestles with the problem of why bad things happen to good people and vice versa. Job's friends argue the traditional view (Deuteronomic Theology) that God grants prosperity to the righteous and punishes the wicked. In the end God, however, appears to Job and clarifies the difference between the wisdom of man and that of God. Through Job's contractions he experienced God and discovered his reality. Job 42: 5-6 reads, "I have heard of thee by the hearing of the ear: but now mine eye seeth thee. Wherefore I abhor myself, and repent in dust and ashes." Job learned that God does things to keep us humble, teach us a lesson or two and prepare us for our purpose. Job in the end, after all that he had gone through; losing it all, his wife speaking foolishly and his friends believing that he had sinned; had to pray for his friends. Job 42:8 reads, "and my servant Job shall pray for you: for him will I accept: lest I deal with you after your folly, in that ye have not spoken of me the thing which is right, like my servant Job." Your contractions are your tests; test position your purpose, vision, dream or destiny to enter into manifestation - the world.

~~~

Through my time of contracting, God put me in a place where it was only him and me. I couldn't depend on my friends in Tallahassee nor could I depend on my family in Plant City. I had to depend on the word that was in me that I and others had planted in me from times past. In the moments where I felt like I couldn't take any more of the troubles I was facing, I started to empathize with Asaph in Psalm 77. Asaph sang, "I cried unto God with my voice, even unto God with my voice; and he gave ear unto me. In the day of my trouble I sought the Lord: my sore ran in the night, and ceased not: my soul refused to be comforted. I remembered God, and was troubled: I complained, and my spirit was overwhelmed. Selah. Thou holdest mine eyes waking: I am so troubled that I cannot speak. I have considered the days of old, the years of ancient times. I call to remembrance my song in the night: I commune with mine own heart: and my spirit made diligent search…I will remember the works of the LORD: surely I will remember thy wonders of old. I will meditate also of all thy work, and talk of thy doings" (Psalm 77:1-6; 11-12).

All during this time of contracting I had to remember the words of God and times of past when He always came through. I had to remember the times when He showed up right on time, when He taught me through experience who

He is, when He showed me my weaknesses and the areas in my character and environment that I had to change. I even remembered the songs of past that helped me keep my mind.

When God places you in a period of trials one after the other you have to think positively and remember the greatness of God and the reason(s) behind your being tried.

When Sarai and Abram had received the promise from God of the birth of their son they began to face many trials because Sarai gave her Egyptian handmaid, Hagar, to her husband. The contractions that she had were actually caused due to the decision she made. Since Sarai didn't hold on to the promise of God and wait for the manifestation, she took matters into her own hands. Now eating on God's promise she had to endure daily contractions seeing the son of Hagar, Ishmael. Even though she later kicked Hagar and Ishmael out of her home, the Lord told Hagar to return. Sarai had to go through this for almost 25 years until she gave birth to her promise, Isaac.

What contractions have you experienced?

How have you reacted in the past when facing test after test?

Is there a song that you find yourself singing when you are going through?

Chapter 8

"But he himself went a day's journey into the wilderness, and came and sat down under a juniper tree: and he requested for himself that he might die; and said, It is enough; now, O LORD, take away my life; for I am not better than my fathers... And he came thither unto a cave, and lodged there; and, behold, the word of the LORD came to him, and he said unto him, What doest thou here, Elijah?"

-I Kings 19: 4:9

Chapter 8: When You Feel Like Quitting

Elijah was a great major prophet who had to experience many trials in order to fulfill the purpose that God had for him. Elijah was a prophet for the Northern Kingdom during the reign of Ahab and he struggled to preserve Israel's worship of God against the corruption by Queen Jezebel and her Phoenician priests of Baal. If you know how evil of a king Ahab was (I Kings 16:30), you can somewhat understand how hard Elijah had to fight and push to live his purpose. Not only did Elijah have to continue on with his purpose fighting against King Ahab, but he had also feared his life because of Queen Jezebel, Ahab's wife. I Kings 19: 1-2 reads, "And Ahab told Jezebel all that Elijah had done, and withal how he had slain all the prophets with the sword. Then Jezebel sent a messenger unto Elijah, saying, So let the gods do to me, and more also, if I make not thy life as the life of one of them by to morrow about this time." Due to this threat Elijah ran away to the wilderness.

I Kings 19:3-4, "And when he saw that, he arose, and went for his life, and came to Beersheba, which belongeth to Judah, and left his servant there. But he himself went a day's journey into the wilderness, and came and sat down under a juniper tree: and he requested for himself that he might die; and said, It is enough; now, O LORD, take away my life; for I am not better than my fathers."

While in the wilderness God sent an angel to Elijah telling him to eat because where God was taking him was "too great" for him (v.7). Elijah eats as he was instructed and later goes 40 days and 40 nights unto Mt. Horeb, the Mount of God. When Elijah stands on Mt. Horeb he experiences strong winds, an earthquake, and a fire, but God was in none of those. After all that, a still small voice comes. The voice of the Lord, "What doest though here, Elijah?" When we take a closer look at the series of events, we realize that Elijah took himself to this wilderness experience, not God. As you read in I Kings 19:3-4, Elijah chose to go to the wilderness alone to die because he was afraid of what man might do to him rather than just believing in God. Instead of Elijah asking God to take his life away, he should have asked the sovereign God for help. But because Elijah was so overwhelmed, he forgot about the power he had within himself.

After hearing the still small voice, God again speaks to Elijah and instructs him to anoint Hazael to be king over Syria (v.15); to anoint Jehu, the son of Nimshi, to be king over Israel; and to anoint Elisha, the son of Shaphat of Abelmeholah, to be prophet "in your room" (v.16). In spite of Elijah's wanting to quit, thinking that he was the only prophet being persecuted and finding shelter under a juniper tree pitying him-self, God was not through with him. Needless to say, Elijah's request for death was denied. He still had to go and anoint men and train them for their purpose.

Elijah went through in order that he may teach the next generation how to endure and overcome the obstacles of the wicked to fulfill God's purpose for their life. God did not feed into Elijah's pity party because He still needed to use him. Elijah's work wasn't done. Elijah's ministry of suffering was for someone else. Every leader is called to be an example and Elijah was called to be an example for the prophets and others.

~~~

When you feel like quitting you have to remember what your God-given purpose is. You have to remember all of the power that you have within yourself. You have to remember the promises of God. When you feel like quitting you can't crawl in a corner and throw a pity party. You cannot throw away your purpose. God will not allow you to anyway because your purpose is the forerunner for someone else's. It was Prophet Elijah who God had wanted to use to ordain Hazael, Jehu, and Elisha. It was Prophet Elijah who God wanted to use to train a host of prophets. It was Prophet Elijah whom He wanted for those times and no one else.

Similarly, God wants to use you and no one else to do a particular, specialized, unique task. Yes, the road may be rough and the days may seem long but if you remember Isaiah 41:13, "For I the Lord thy God will hold thy right hand, saying unto thee, Fear not; I will help thee," then in times of despair and moments of weariness, you can encourage yourself and ask God for help. When you are at high points in your life and it seems to be going well, you need to be filling yourself with the word of God. Because when you get to your lows, you need to be able to draw from the word and strength from within yourself.

While on my journey of fulfilling my purpose on earth, there were many times when I wanted to quit. I was tired of constantly going through, facing trials that I didn't understand, having people lie about me and mistreat me, feeling always alone while standing in a large crowd, wanting never to get close to anyone because God would always allow me to feel that person's burden. At the same time I never really had the opportunity to address my hurts only because I was always helping others with theirs. Please understand, by all means, I am not complaining. I am a counselor at heart and having not one child I truly have the spirit of a mother. But I always wanted to find someone who I could release my hurts and burdens to. However, through this 15-month season of preparation and contractions, God has definitely made it crystal clear that He is the one and only one I am supposed to release to.

At some point, a few years ago, I found myself wanting to have a mentor because I thought that was the "thing" and I used to ask for certain people to mentor me but it never worked. God always did something to break that connection. When people started to approach me and ask me if I would mentor them I would most of the time say yes, but because I was intrigued by this whole international mentorship movement that was going on, and because I was mentoring individuals, I thought that it would be best for me to find a mentor for myself. Since that (my having a mentor figure) never worked out, I ended up realizing that I was probably like Paul in the sense of being taught by God and not by man. I was so stuck on man mentoring me so that I could make sure I was affectively and properly mentoring others to where God closed that avenue for a while.

Galatians 1:15-19, "But when it pleased God, who separated me from my mother's womb, and called me by his grace, To reveal his Son in me, that I might preach him among the heathen; immediately I conferred not with flesh and blood: Neither went I up to Jerusalem to them which were apostles before me; but I went into Arabia, and returned again unto Damascus. Then after three years I went up to Jerusalem to see Peter, and abode with him fifteen days. But other of the apostles saw I none, save James the Lord's brother." (Read also Galatians 2:1-10).

So when I go through and when I feel like quitting I have to think about all the people who God has connected to me. I have to remember the things of old and hold on to who I know God to be.

Four years ago I had a dream that I was at a church conference in a gymnasium and a bad storm had fell on the area. Everyone who was in the gymnasium started to run outside to get into their cars and head back to the designated hotel but when they got outside the doors of the gymnasium, they all stopped abruptly because they thought the storm was too strong to run through or drive in. I was standing almost all the way in the back of the crowd. Eventually, I started to make my way through the crowd because I said to myself, "Imma make a run for it." Well, when I got through the crowd I started running, and then suddenly I was flying in the air (as stated in a few chapters back, when faced with obstacles in my dreams I fly over or around them). So, while flying in the air, lightening strikes three times and each time a bolt would hit a tree and the tree would fall somewhere relatively close by me. I ended up making it back to the hotel, but instead of walking in when I landed, I walked to the last tree that had fallen. I climbed inside of the tree and looked up to see God looking down at me. He asked, "What?" in an authoritative tone. I began to explain to him how I felt about the storm, the lightening and the trees falling near me. He then replied, "It's just a storm." And then I woke up. So when I get frustrated with the storms, which are needed due to my purpose, I tell myself, "It's just a storm."

~~~

A week ago while writing this chapter, I emailed my Pastor and First Lady and told them that I needed a break from the church because I had gotten tired of dealing with everything associated with my purpose. I reassured them that I wasn't moving, joining another church, nor starting one. I just really needed a break! For a month straight I had been up every night until 3:00 a.m. or 5:00 a.m., and I kept having dream after dream. If I wasn't sleep, I kept having vision after vision. I had to keep telling myself that I wasn't going to lose my mind. I'm a strong believer that something happens (or changes) to a person when they don't get enough hours of sleep at night. I was physically tired as well as spiritually tired. I was unintentionally separating myself from people. At times, I intentionally tried to avoid people and keep to myself because I didn't want God to show me anything about anyone. But don't you know God got smart? This was my first time ever experiencing anything like what I'm about to tell you. For two nights straight I had dreams of me stepping into other people's dreams and prophesying to them. I would wake up in the morning drained more than ever, as if I had actually walked around a church prophesying to people. It was as if God had said, "If you won't do it willingly then I'll wait until you fall asleep." God was up to some new things.

Getting back to the email, I even told my Pastor that I would give him back my ordination I.D. card and certificate. I was even planning on giving him the key back to the church. I mean I wanted a full break. I felt like I needed to rest, heal myself and break away from everybody and their issues. Am I the only preacher that has ever felt like this?

For anybody who knows my Pastor, he didn't respond right away to the email; he never does. He waited until the next day to call and let me know how he felt about the situation and he asked me a few questions. I had basically let him talk because I was just tired and stubborn and I needed an "outsider's" view or response to my birthing experience. After a while, he let me know that he wasn't going to allow me to take a break nor was he taking back my I.D. card, certificate and key because "all that is yours," he said. But there is one thing he said to me that rung in my ear after we got off the phone and that was, "don't take it personal."

Now at first I almost yelled at him and asked, "what do you mean don't take it personal?" In my mind I had lost everything, and it's been a month since I had a peaceful night's rest. Hello! I was experiencing this, not him. I'm so serious. I almost got mad. Almost. But God changed my thinking very quickly.

I'm not going through because I did anything wrong; I'm going through to position my purpose for birthing and to, like Elijah, encourage others, perhaps some young, aspiring prophets and prophetesses, who are (or will be) experiencing this same journey to endure through it all. I know without a doubt that God is transforming me to handle where He is taking me. Just as the angel told Elijah, "arise and eat; because the journey is too great for thee." I have to accept every trial as a tool to make me stronger for what's ahead and so do you.

Have you ever felt like quitting?

Who do you talk to when you feel like you can't take anymore?

What verses in the Bible sustains you during most of your trials?

Chapter 9

"Then the word of the LORD came unto me, saying, Before I formed thee in the belly I knew thee; and before thou camest forth out of the womb I sanctified thee, and I ordained thee a prophet unto the nations. Then said I, Ah, Lord GOD! behold, I cannot speak: for I am a child. But the LORD said unto me, Say not, I am a child: for thou shalt go to all that I shall send thee, and whatsoever I command thee thou shalt speak. Be not afraid of their faces: for I am with thee to deliver thee, saith the LORD. Then the LORD put forth his hand, and touched my mouth. And the LORD said unto me, Behold, I have put my words in thy mouth. See, I have this day set thee over the nations and over the kingdoms, to root out, and to pull down, and to destroy, and to throw down, to build, and to plant."

-Jeremiah 1:4-10

Chapter 9: Reasons Why You Shouldn't Quit Pushing

The most important reason why you shouldn't quit pushing is because God put something in you, not for your self glory, but for someone else. If you have gone through all the processes of preparation and positioning, there really is no need to quit at the end. It is more painful and depressing to have a still born resting in your womb because either way, it has to come out; there will be no fruitfulness from this type of birthing experience. So don't kill what God has put in you.

In the beginning God told Jeremiah what he would be doing. He told Jeremiah that he would be set "over the nations and over the kingdoms, to root out, and to pull down, and to destroy, and to throw down, to build and to plant" (Jeremiah 1:10). Jeremiah had a large and heavy purpose. God even warned him to not be afraid of people's faces and He reassures him that He will be with him as well as deliver him. As stated in the last chapter, don't take it personal, God just wants to use you.

Jeremiah was one of the greatest prophets ever. He was the son of a priest, Hilkiah, and a native of Anathoth. Jeremiah was in ministry for 40 years, from the middle of King Josiah's reign to the fall of Jerusalem. When called by God, Jeremiah's mouth was touched by God's hand, and when God had touched Jeremiah's mouth, God said, "I have put my words in thy mouth" (Jeremiah 1:9). Later, Jeremiah was told his mission and purpose: to protest against the sinfulness and folly of his countrymen, especially Judah's kings and leaders. Jeremiah eventually attacked the prevalent belief that the very existence of the temple, thought to be the home of God, was a guarantee of national security (Jeremiah 7:1-15). Jeremiah instead insisted that true social behavior and faithfulness to God is the only sure reliance of security. Because God had put His words in the mouth of Jeremiah, Jeremiah had no choice but to be outspoken about certain topics. Even though Jeremiah was outspoken for God he nearly lost his life (Jeremiah 26) and after the fall of Jerusalem, Jeremiah's friends strongly encouraged him to flee with them to Egypt (Jeremiah 40-43).

Now you may be thinking that this isn't a great example of a reason to not quit pushing, but it actually is. Jeremiah wanted to quit on several occasions, but he couldn't due to the effect it would have on the people. Jeremiah had to keep speaking the words of God in spite of threats, mistreatment, being misunderstood and being alone. Remember, God had put His words in Jeremiah's mouth.

Paul writes in II Timothy 3:10-12, "But thou hast fully known my doctrine, manner of life, purpose, faith, longsuffering, charity, patience, Persecutions, afflictions, which came unto me at Antioch, at Iconium, at Lystra; what persecutions I endured: but out of them all the Lord delivered me. Yea, and all that will live godly in Christ Jesus shall suffer persecution." Regardless of if you are pushing or not, you will face persecution. So why not push with every contraction (test) that comes? Why not push in order to birth what's inside of you? As it is written in God's word, if you want to reign with Him you will have to suffer for Him. As James 1:2 states, "my brethren, count it all joy when ye fall into divers temptation." God simply wants to use you as his vessel, His mouthpiece. Question is, will you let Him?

~~~

Every time I think about quitting I think about all the people who will be affected. I think about my mentees, my nieces and nephews, and even the people whom I haven't met yet. And more than anything else, I think of how God would feel if I would quit on Him. He went to the cross and suffered more for me more than I will ever experience for Him. So for me being His child; quitting on my father just doesn't seem right. What do you think?

Reasons to not quit pushing

- For the growth of God's kingdom

- Because Jesus didn't quit

- For your health

- To help someone else

- To live with purpose

- Because you were chosen by God
- You are strong enough
- To bring change
- To prepare the way for someone else
- God put something in you to be birthed

Who can you depend on to encourage you?

Have you ever felt like quitting on your purpose?

How do you think God would feel if you quit?

Chapter 10

"Now Elisabeth's full time came that she should be delivered; and she brought forth a son... And so it was, that, while they were there, the days were accomplished that she should be delivered."

-Luke 1:57; 2:6

Chapter 10: Birthing God's Purpose For Your Life

It has been a little over two years ago since a good friend of mine had my godson. I made sure I would be able to leave work and head to the hospital the day she would go in labor. While at work, I got the text to head to the hospital because her contractions started coming more frequently. When I arrived to the hospital everything appeared to be calm and slow moving. For about 30 minutes nothing happened. We were all in the delivery room talking about our day, reminiscing about the past nine months and discussing how preparations were made for this big day. While in the middle of a sentence my friend said that she felt the need to push so we all rushed out of the room to summon the doctor. Within three minutes a nurse walked into the waiting area and said "Kita?" I looked at her. I tried to figure out why she called for me and she simply said, "they need you." Now I'm stunned because I'm thinking "the daddy in there, what they need me for." But I got up and followed the nurse into the room. The daddy immediately directed me to the camera and told me to videotape everything. This was something I did not sign up for; I didn't major in video production! I simply agreed to be the godmother. Who knew that all this was involved in accepting the role as godmother?

This experience I will never forget. While in the delivery room, I was standing to the left side of the bed videotaping, as instructed, as well as encouraging my friend to push whenever she started to get tired. I was her bedside cheerleader. When the doctor finally said "the head is out," it seemed that weight was lifted off of everyone in the room. When my godson was fully birthed, and took his first gulp of air, I noticed that the work was still far from over because even though the promise and the purpose was birthed, the individual who was in labor still had to release the afterbirth, which is what nurtures and secures the fetus while in the womb. This experience made me think I could be a nurse.

For the last 15 months I can honestly say that I have been through every level of being prepared and positioned to birth the purpose God put in me. I am most definitely assured that I will be relieved when my labor is over.

I really want to thank those who were allowed to assist me during this journey and I want to thank God for trusting me with such a major purpose. I am ready to push! How about you?

~~~

When you are in your delivery room being prepped to give birth to your purpose, you have to make sure that the right people are in the room with you. You can't allow just anyone in there. You need a solid, consistent support team.

You should already know what purpose, vision or dream you have been called to birth so when manifestation time comes you will be able to name it what God already told you to name it. No one else can name your purpose for you. Just like when Elizabeth gave birth to John, an angel had already told her what to name the child. As a result, tradition was broken and change had begun to take place. Question, are you ready to give birth?

You have endured sleepless nights, a change of lifestyle, your character has been tested, you have faced unexpected trials, you started losing one thing after the next, you wanted to quit, but you had to remember things of old, and now you must identify encouragers to surround yourself with, those who are faithful and consistent, who will be available to stand by your side in the delivery room, who will not let you stop pushing until you have given birth.

God allowed you to go through tests, trials, and tribulations to strengthen you, to equip you, to prepare you and to position you for kingdom work. All that you have been (or are going) through was for a particular reason.

There are some people who need you to push. Their lives depend on you! Whether you want to believe it or not, your purpose is someone else's life line. In order for someone to start their journey to their wilderness experience, you have to give birth to your purpose. Many times, in order for someone to know that they can make it, they have to see you make it first. You can't quit now; it's almost time to push!

But before you push you have to make sure you have made all the proper arrangements.

You need to know where your purpose will be used. Don't push if you are just going to let your purpose sit on the shelf. If you place your purpose on the shelf, or leave it unattended for too long, then you would have went though all that pain in vain. You would essentially be neglecting what God gave you. This is called purpose abuse. Don't abuse your purpose, dream or vision. It needs a home, it needs to be nurtured and it needs to be used. So question, where are you going to use your purpose?

A lot of times individuals have a lot of things going on in any particular day so they ask for a purpose-sitter. Have you delegated a person or persons to help you with your purpose? Sometimes you can't watch after and check the status of your purpose on any given day; on some days it may not be your priority. So you need to make sure to have a support system in place, people who will help you carry your purpose, vision or dream, with as much care and sincerity as you do. Some people birth visions whereas for others, they are called to care for visions and make sure they mature. So question, who do you have lined up?

Well, if you have everything in order and people in place, then now the time has come for you to push!

Brace yourself for the birthing of your purpose and make sure that you never quit pushing. Push yourself to keep your purpose alive. Push yourself to new heights in God. Push yourself to be the best person God has ordained and birthed you to be. Remember that with God all things are possible, so don't quit in life when things get hard. Just keep pushing!

Closing Scripture

"Before she travailed, she brought forth; before her pain came, she was delivered of a man child. Who hath heard such a thing? who hath seen such things? Shall the earth be made to bring forth in one day? or shall a nation be born at once? for as soon as Zion travailed, she brought forth her children. Shall I bring to the birth, and not cause to bring forth? saith the LORD: shall I cause to bring forth, and shut the womb? saith thy God. Rejoice ye with Jerusalem, and be glad with her, all ye that love her: rejoice for joy with her, all ye that mourn for her: That ye may suck, and be satisfied with the breasts of her consolations; that ye may milk out, and be delighted with the abundance of her glory. For thus saith the LORD, Behold, I will extend peace to her like a river, and the glory of the Gentiles like a flowing stream: then shall ye suck, ye shall be borne upon her sides, and be dandled upon her knees. As one whom his mother comforteth, so will I comfort you; and ye shall be comforted in Jerusalem. And when ye see this, your heart shall rejoice, and your bones shall flourish like an herb: and the hand of the LORD shall be known toward his servants, and his indignation toward his enemies."

-Isaiah 66:7-14

The Author

Minister Chakita Hargrove grew up in Plant City, Florida where she attended Greater New Hope AMPRC under the pastorship of Calvin E. Callins, Sr. She moved to Tallahassee, Florida in June 2002 and received her Bachelor's of Arts degree in Humanities and Religious Studies from the renowned Florida State University in Summer 2006. She later received her Certification in Pre-Kindergarten Disabilities. During her stay in Tallahassee, she accepted her call to preach and teach in October 2004. She was formally announced to the congregation in January 2005 and delivered her initial sermon, "Break Yourself," on August 28, 2005.

Currently, Minister Hargrove resides in Hillsborough County where she is actively involved in the ministries of Greater New Hope AMPRC, Elder Calvin Earl Callins, Sr., Pastor. At Greater New Hope, Minister Hargrove serves as Editor-in-Chief of the *Greater New Hope Herald*, a church newsletter publication product of *Heart.Ink Press, LLC,* and as the Minister of Administration. On January 18, 2009, she was ordained as Minister Prophetess Chakita Hargrove under the tutelage of Elder Callins, Sr.

She is a God fearing woman and a committed servant of the Lord. Many people respect her for being righteous and honest. Already, she holds several persons under her wings who look to her as a spiritual counselor and mentor. Minister Hargrove has a passion for the spiritual wellness of God's children and when the Spirit of the Living God told her to launch Heart of Man Ministries (HOMM), Inc.; so she did. God has birthed Heart of Man Ministries through her because of the faith and love she has for the Word of God and for the children of God. Minister Hargrove is CEO of both HOMM and *Heart.Ink Press, LLC,* a unique publishing expansion of HOMM. Minister Hargrove is also an active member of Zeta Phi Beta Sorority, Incorporated.

Chakita Hargrove
Heart of Man Ministries, Inc.
PO Box 6312
Tallahassee, FL 32314

www.heartofmanministries.com
Chakita.hargrove@heartofmanministries.com

Pregnant? Push!: Birthing God's Purpose For Your Life
Additional Copies are available at
www.heartinkpress.com

Other Authored Work

Calling All Disciples: Growing in Christ
Cost: $8.00

Are you ready to go higher in your spiritual walk with Christ? Are you serious about becoming a disciple for Christ? If so, this is the handbook for you! Various topics, sixteen total, are gathered together in one book to help believers in Christ grow to their God-given potential. Topics consist of, with scriptural references, Forgiveness, Communion, the Holy Spirit, Discipleship, Tithes, Evangelism and much more.

www.heartinkpress.com/library.html

Heart.Ink Press, LLC

PO Box 6312

Tallahassee, FL 32314

www.ingramcontent.com/pod-product-compliance
Lightning Source LLC
Chambersburg PA
CBHW062004040426
42447CB00010B/1912